The Red Vest

Little Bunny got a new red vest that fit just right. Little Mouse saw it and liked it, so he borrowed it to wear.
"It looks nice, but it's a bit big and a bit long."

Then Little Dog saw the vest and borrowed it, too.
"Not bad, but it's a bit small and a bit short."

Little Bunny wore the red vest to visit Little Sheep, who also had a red vest. Together, the tall and short friends started to dance.

Then Little Elephant joined in with his red vest, and they all danced together.

The Flowing River

Water flows down from high places.

Pebbles sink to the riverbed,

Fish swim in the river,

And leaves and little boats float along the stream.